VICTORIAN HOUSES
ARCHITECTURE COLORING BOOK

A. G. SMITH

DOVER PUBLICATIONS
GARDEN CITY, NEW YORK

The Victorian era was a period of profound social change, and many of these upheavals were reflected in the building styles of the time. Styles of architecture of this period—created for the more affluent and spread by imitation by the rapidly expanding middle class—were characterized by a romantic impulse. Thirty-one meticulously detailed renderings illustrate many distinctive Victorian styles and their often elaborate embellishments. This collection showcases the formal evolution of the Victorian home, from the earliest Gothic Revival structures of the 1830s and '40s to the grandest "cottages" of the Gilded Age. The pages have been perforated here, so displaying your finished art is easy!

Copyright

Copyright © 1983, 2001 by A. G. Smith
Copyright © 2016 by Dover Publications
All rights reserved.

Bibliographical Note

Victorian Houses Architecture Coloring Book, first published by Dover Publications in 2016, is a republication in one volume of all twenty-nine plates from the previously published Dover book, *Victorian Houses* (2001), and two plates from *The American House Styles of Architecture Coloring Book* (1983).

International Standard Book Number

ISBN-13: 978-0-486-80794-2
ISBN-10: 0-486-80794-0

Manufactured in the United States of America
80794011   2021
www.doverpublications.com

The Russell-Cooper House, Mount Vernon, Ohio, 1829, renovated 1890. Here is a fine example of Midwestern Eclectic: a simple clapboard box overlaid with Italianate-Moorish details, and painted in bright, cheerful colors.

A house in Portland, Maine, from a design by A. J. Downing, 1840s. Downing (1815-52) was America's first great landscape architect and a prolific writer who promoted the virtues of the freestanding house in a "natural," picturesque setting. Vaux and Olmsted, the designers of Central Park and other great urban parks and early garden suburbs, were directly influenced by his ideas. This house is based on his "Cottage in the English or Rural Gothic Style."

A villa in the Pointed (Gothic Revival) style, Albany, New York, c.1840. This design is by A. J. Davis (1803-92), a chief promoter of the Picturesque aesthetic early in the nineteenth century, promulgator of both the Greek and Gothic Revival styles, mentor of A. J. Downing, and co-founder of America's first professional architectural firm.

Bellevue House, Kingston, Ontario, 1840s. This is one of the few examples of early Victorian Italianate architecture in Canada. It was once the home of John A. MacDonald, Canada's first prime minister.

An Alpine style cottage, Tolland, Connecticut, c.1840s. More modest than the "ornamental German" country house (no. 14), this small house has a simple basic form decorated with a scrollwork balcony and roof brackets, and seems to show some Italianate influence.

Font Hill, Riverdale, New York, 1849. This highly theatrical crenellated structure, consisting of six interlocked octagonal towers, was built by the famous tragedian Edwin Forrest early in the Victorian period, when the Romantic influence was at its strongest. (He borrowed the name from Fonthill Abbey, a famous English house also known as "Beckford's Folly.") When the house was completed, Forrest celebrated by staging a "medieval entertainment" for the workers.

Octagon House, Ottawa, Illinois, 1856. In 1849 Orson Fowler, a phrenologist, publisher, and sexual reformer (among other professions), published *A Home for All*, in which he advocated the building of octagonal houses, on the grounds that they made better use of space. Fowler also advocated central heating and indoor toilets. The book was a bestseller, and many octagonal houses were built in the 1850s.

A small clapboard house with Italianate windows and a pagoda-style roof, Kalamazoo, Michigan, 1865. This vernacular style might be called Midwestern Eclectic: it demonstrates a certain self-confident American freedom to appropriate and adapt whatever the designer—most likely, in this case, the homeowner himself—finds appealing.

A cottage villa design by Gervase Wheeler, 1867. Wheeler, an English architect who worked with A. J. Downing, was a leading exponent of the Picturesque, which featured rustic dwellings in carefully arranged "natural" settings. Here he has adapted an earlier Gothic Revival style to a somewhat later taste, with both covered and uncovered verandas, an Italianate balustrade, and a fanciful roofline.

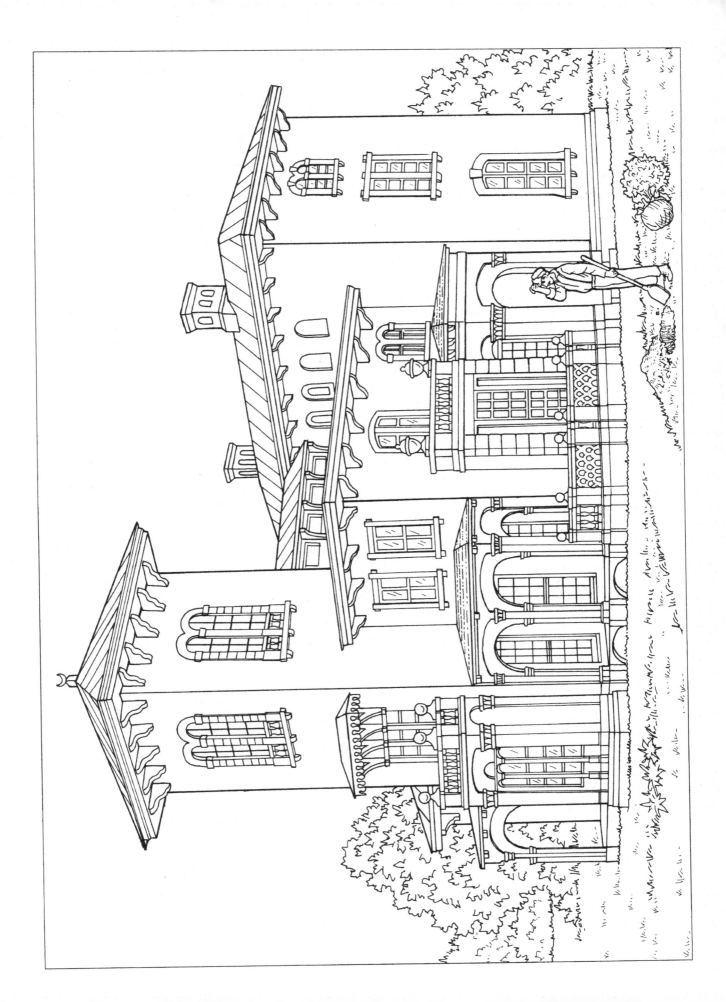

An Italianate villa design by Gervase Wheeler, 1867. This house has the classic square tower, tall windows, asymmetry and simplicity of design that characterizes the earlier Victorian Italianate style.

The Watkins-Coleman House, Midway, Utah, 1868. Basically Gothic, with its steep gables and fanciful scrollwork, this house is built of abundant local material: painted adobe brick and sandstone.

The "Pink House," Wellsville, New York, 1868. This house has the square tower and tall, narrow windows typical of the Italianate villa, along with much gingerbread ornamentation. The house is painted bright pink with white trim, according to the original owner's wishes.

High-Victorian Gothic, Earlville, New York, c.1875. This style combines all the elements of the earlier Gothic styles—the pointed Gothic windows, the Italianate tower, stickwork in the gable, and a liberal application of frilly ironwork. The single most characteristic feature of the High-Victorian Gothic style was elaborate coloration, achieved through the use of varied materials on single surfaces and by painting the walls and trim with highly contrasting colors and tones. This approach differs greatly from the muted coloration of the early Gothic Revival houses.

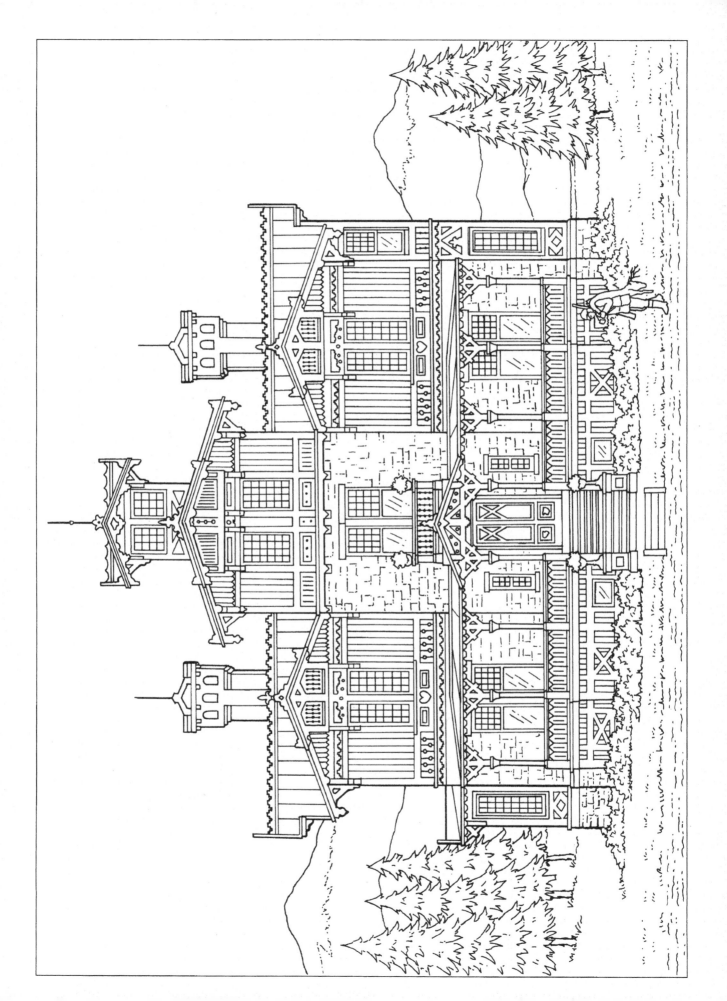

A country house in an "ornamental German" style, 1877. Intended to be constructed of stone and wood, this design represents a departure from the more usual English, Italian, or French derivations of Victorian house design. It is just as elaborately decorated, however. Despite appearances, this house does not resemble a cuckoo clock: cuckoo clocks are designed to resemble houses like this.

A "double cottage" in the Second Empire style, 1877. This is a design for an undivided house to be shared by two families. The floor plan is complete with two kitchens and two dining rooms, but fails to provide for even one bathroom or W.C., a rather puzzling omission.

A modest Second Empire house with elaborate ornamentation, from a pattern book, 1878. Notice the effect of the combination of the concave profile of the mansard roof with the convex curve of the cupola.

The John Anderton House, Chicopee Falls, Massachusetts, 1879. The Second Empire style was inspired by the grand buildings erected in the rebuilt Paris of the Second Empire period (1852-1870). Its most characteristic feature is the mansard roof with dormer windows and cast-iron decorative cresting. Second Empire became the most popular style for public buildings in the United States after the Civil War and was also employed in large and ostentatious private residences. Here it is adapted to lend distinction to a somewhat less grandiose home.

The Gaylord Residence, Chicopee Falls, Massachusetts, 1879. Another eclectic mix of Victorian styles, primarily Italianate, with unusual massed columns supporting the veranda roofs.

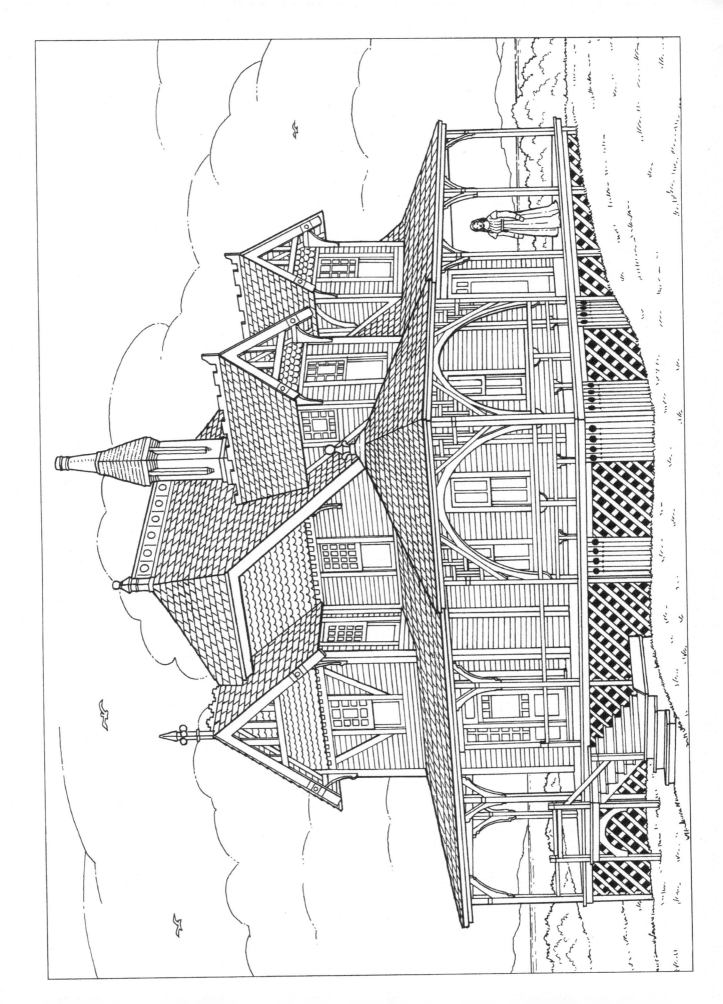

A seaside cottage in the Stick style, 1881. Stick style—an outgrowth of Victorian Gothic—was popular from the 1850s to the 1870s and was characterized by asymmetry, angular masses, colored shingles, exposed "structural" (actually decorative) beams, decorative brackets, and other "stickwork." (The name "Stick style" was applied retrospectively in the twentieth century.)

Vinland (the Catherine Lorillard Wolfe Residence), Newport, Rhode Island, 1882-84. The design of this Gilded Age "cottage" shows the clear influence of the architect H. H. Richardson (1838-86). Richardson developed a very distinctive and influential style based on the Romanesque, employing rough-cut masonry, large circular arches, recessed windows, and short, heavy columns to achieve an effect of monumental strength and stability in large urban houses and public buildings.

A village residence, from a pattern book, 1885. A further variation on the Stick style, a version of the Gothic.

The Carson Mansion, Eureka, California, 1885. This fantastic house, an eclectic. not to say eccentric. mixture of styles, was built by a Northern California lumber baron. Constructed primarily of redwood, it also uses exotic woods from South America. the Philippines. the East Indies. and Mexico. The house features "aggressively frightful" ornamental carving and stained glass representations of characters from Shakespeare. As one writer put it, it has become famous because it is "almost a parody on a Victorian house."

Urban houses in the Moorish style, Baltimore, Maryland, 1886. In addition to the lasting influence throughout the Victorian period in Gothic, Italian, and French building models, there were a number of other, somewhat more exotic, sources of historical form and decoration. Among them was Moorish architecture, characterized by pointed arches, domes, minaret-type spires, and colorful tile mosaics. Though never as widespread as other historicizing types, the Moorish fit comfortably with the Victorian interest in dramatic, romantic architectural form.

The Washburn Residence, Boston, Massachusetts, 1880. This substantial townhouse also shows the Richardson influence, though it lacks the massive, dense monumentality of Richardson's own large masonry houses.

A Chicago, Illinois, row house, 1880s. Here a Richardsonian element, the semidetached cylindrical tower, has been grafted (in truncated form) onto an otherwise ordinary row house in an apparent effort to make it more imposing. The lightweight wooden porch rather contradicts the effect, though.

An Italianate residence, San Francisco, California, 1880s. The Italianate style, seen earlier mostly in freestanding "villas," was adapted for the ubiquitous urban row houses that appeared in the post-Civil War era. This row house, or brownstone, style is characterized by the sort of elaborate decorative elements seen here: columned doorways, heavily detailed, often arched window and door treatments, balustraded stair railings and occasional decorative balconies, and elaborate molded cornices (often of cast iron) with scrolled brackets.

A Queen Anne style house, 1880s. The Queen Anne style was an eclectic successor to the Gothic, incorporating features from a variety of sources and emphasizing comfort over historicizing consistency. Characteristic features include facades with arches, projections, and balconies; gable ends with sculptural decorations; fluted chimneys, and patterned shingling.

The Warren Weston House, Chappaquiddick Island, Massachusetts, c.1880s. This is an example of the Shingle style, an eclectic, uniquely American style whose best and most characteristic examples are large seaside "cottages" in the Gilded Age resorts of New England, New York, and New Jersey. Even more than the Queen Anne, the Shingle style was unlimited by conformity to historicizing ideas; spaces tended to be flowing and full of natural light from many large windows. Its most distinct features are its asymmetric masses and textured exterior surfaces, composed, of course, of shingles, on walls, columns, and roofs.

A stone-and-shingle suburban, Tuxedo Park, New York, 1888. Another large Gilded Age "cottage" that shows a Richardson influence.

"Steamboat" or Carpenter Gothic: a modest house with elaborate decoration, Southbridge, Massachusetts, 1890s. Carpenter Gothic was made possible by the invention of the scroll saw, or jigsaw, which enabled any skilled carpenter to create fanciful decorative brackets, perforated "bargeboards," and other ornamental woodwork at low cost, transforming ordinary boxlike houses into gingerbread delights. This one is a fairly restrained example.

Queen Anne, Los Angeles Historical Society, Los Angeles, California, c.1890.
The Queen Anne style, the first of the "surface styles," was popular in America from the late 1870s through the 1890s. Variety of form, color, texture, and materials distinguishes the style. A single house may combine stone, shingles, brick, and half-timbering, with accents of Gothic, Renaissance, and Romanesque detail. All this may be topped off with a massive chimney paneled in molded brick. Bay windows and gabled porches were frequently used, as were turrets during the latter stages of the style's development. Windows could be either round or flat-topped, and stained glass was often used in stairwells and in transoms above windows and doors.